Manatees

by Ann Herriges

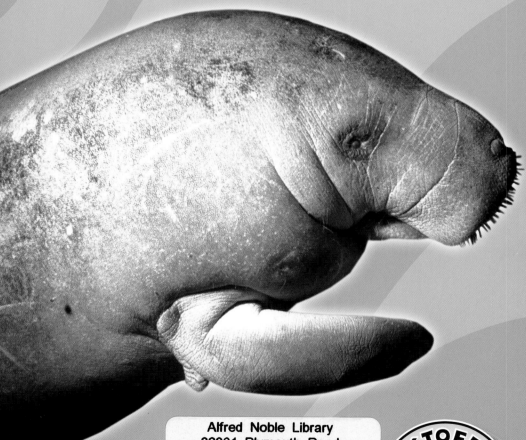

BLASTOFF! READERS
2

BELLWETHER MEDIA • MINNEAPOLIS, MN

JUL 1 7 2007

Note to Librarians, Teachers, and Parents:

Blastoff! Readers are carefully developed by literacy experts and combine standards-based content with developmentally appropriate text.

Level 1 provides the most support through repetition of high-frequency words, light text, predictable sentence patterns, and strong visual support.

Level 2 offers early readers a bit more challenge through varied simple sentences, increased text load, and less repetition of high-frequency words.

Level 3 advances early-fluent readers toward fluency through increased text and concept load, less reliance on visuals, longer sentences, and more literary language.

Whichever book is right for your reader, Blastoff! Readers are the perfect books to build confidence and encourage a love of reading that will last a lifetime!

This edition first published in 2007 by Bellwether Media.

No part of this publication may be reproduced in whole or in part without written permission of the publisher. For information regarding permission, write to Bellwether Media Inc., Attention: Permissions Department, Post Office Box 1C, Minnetonka, MN 55345-9998.

Library of Congress Cataloging-in-Publication Data
Herriges, Ann.
    Manatees / by Ann Herriges.
        p. cm. — (Blastoff! readers) (Oceans alive!)
Summary: "Simple text and supportive images introduce beginning readers to manatees. Intended for students in kindergarten through third grade."
    Includes bibliographical references and index.
    ISBN-10: 1-60014-048-3 (hardcover : alk. paper)
    ISBN-13: 978-1-60014-048-8 (hardcover : alk. paper)
    1. Manatees—Juvenile literature. I. Title. II. Series. III. Series: Oceans alive!

    QL737.S63H47 2007
    599.55—dc22   2006003136

Text copyright © 2007 by Bellwether Media.
Printed in the United States of America.

Table of Contents

The manatee is a large **mammal**. It is as big as a car.

The manatee swims slowly in warm waters.

The manatee has a small head and a short neck.

Its mouth and nose are called the **snout**. **Whiskers** grow on the snout.

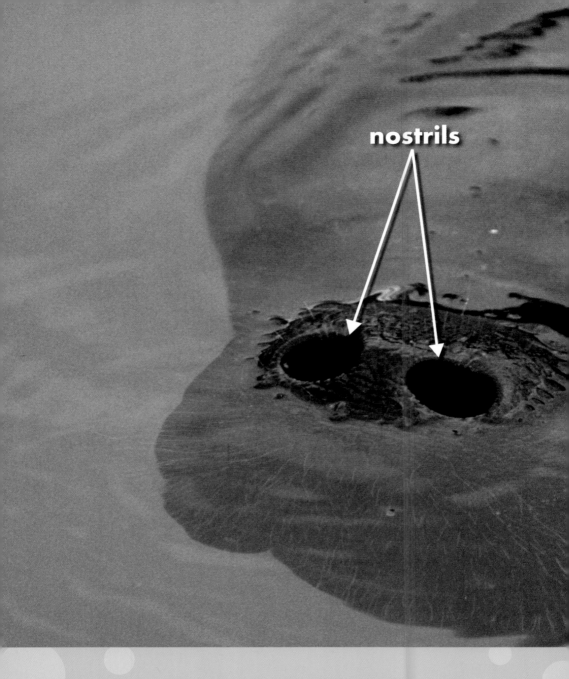

nostrils

The manatee has two **nostrils** on top of its snout.

The manatee pokes its nostrils out of the water to breathe air.

The manatee has big lips.

The manatee has small
eyes that are far apart.

tail

The manatee's body is round and **wrinkled**.

Its tail is flat and wide. The manatee moves its tail up and down to swim.

The manatee has two **flippers**. The flippers help the manatee steer.

flippers

The manatee has flat nails at the end of each flipper.

The manatee **migrates** in winter. It leaves the ocean to feed in warmer river waters.

The manatee looks for water plants to eat.

The manatee uses its flippers to dig up plant **roots**. It grinds plants with its flat teeth.

18

Then the manatee cleans its teeth. It uses its flippers or rolls sand around in its mouth.

19

Manatees make sounds to find each other in the water.

Then it's time to play!

Glossary

flipper—a wide, flat limb that some ocean animals use to swim

mammal—an animal with a backbone that is warm-blooded and has hair; mammals are born alive and drink their mother's milk.

migrate—to move from one place to another; manatees live near the ocean shore most of the year; they migrate to rivers when the ocean becomes cold in winter.

nostrils—openings in the nose used for breathing; manatees have flaps on their nostrils that they can close when they are underwater.

roots—the part of a plant that grows under the ground

snout—the front part of an animal's head that makes up the nose, mouth, and jaw

whiskers—stiff hairs that grow near an animal's mouth

wrinkle—lines or folds in the skin

To Learn More

AT THE LIBRARY

Andreae, Giles. *Commotion in the Ocean*. Wilton, Conn.: Tiger Tales, 2002.

Jacobs, Francine. *Sam the Sea Cow*. New York: Walker, 1991.

Lithgow, John. *I'm a Manatee*. New York: Simon & Schuster, 2003.

McNulty, Faith. *Dancing with Manatees*. New York: Scholastic, 1994.

Staub, Frank. *Manatees*. Minneapolis, Minn.: Lerner Publications, 1998.

ON THE WEB

Learning more about manatees is as easy as 1, 2, 3.

1. Go to www.factsurfer.com

2. Enter "manatees" into search box.

3. Click the "Surf" button and you will see a list of related web sites.

With factsurfer.com, finding more information is just a click away.

Index

The photographs in this book are reproduced through the courtesy of: Cousteau Society/Getty Images, front cover; David Hosking/Alamy, pp. 4-5; Brian Skerry/Getty Images, p. 6; Brandon Cole Marine Photography/Alamy, p. 7; Andre Seale/Alamy, pp. 8-9; Michael Aw/Getty Images, p. 10; Peter Arnold, Inc./Alamy, pp. 11, 14-15, 18-19, 20-21; Wolfgang Polzer/Alamy, pp. 12-13; Peter Pearson/Getty Images, pp. 16-17.